How Animals Change: The Interaction of Animals and Scientists

by Samuel D. Gorey

Editorial Offices: Glenview, Illinois • Parsippany, New Jersey • New York, New York
Sales Offices: Needham, Massachusetts • Duluth, Georgia • Glenview, Illinois
Coppell, Texas • Ontario, California • Mesa, Arizona

Every effort has been made to secure permission and provide appropriate credit for photographic material. The publisher deeply regrets any omission and pledges to correct errors called to its attention in subsequent editions.

Unless otherwise acknowledged, all photographs are the property of Scott Foresman, a division of Pearson Education.

Photo locators denoted as follows: Top (T), Center (C), Bottom (B), Left (L), Right (R), Background (Bkgd)

Opener: Corbis; 1 ©Dorling Kindersley; 3 ©Dorling Kindersley; 4 (Inset) ©Dorling Kindersley, (B) Corbis; 6 ©Dorling Kindersley; 8 ©Dorling Kindersley; 9 Brand X Pictures; 10 Brand X Pictures; 11 Brand X Pictures; 12 ©Dorling Kindersley; 13 ©Dorling Kindersley; 15 ©Dorling Kindersley; 16 Corbis; 18 ©Dorling Kindersley; 19 ©Dorling Kindersley; 21 ©Dorling Kindersley; 22 ©Dorling Kindersley; 23 ©Dorling Kindersley

ISBN: 0-328-13641-7

Copyright © Pearson Education, Inc.

All Rights Reserved. Printed in the United States of America. This publication is protected by Copyright, and permission should be obtained from the publisher prior to any prohibited reproduction, storage in a retrieval system, or transmission in any form by any means, electronic, mechanical, photocopying, recording, or likewise. For information regarding permission(s), write to: Permissions Department, Scott Foresman, 1900 East Lake Avenue, Glenview, Illinois 60025.

1 2 3 4 5 6 7 8 9 10 V0G1 14 13 12 11 10 09 08 07 06 05

What about the animals?

Wild animals are studied by researchers all over the world for a variety of reasons. For instance, researchers may develop medicines from the cells of wild animals, which doctors can then use to treat diseases.

It is easy to see how the study of wild animals impacts our lives, most often in favorable ways, as is the case with medicines. But how easy is it for us to see how wild animals themselves are affected by our studies? After all, with few exceptions, wild animals cannot communicate to us what changes they experience when they are analyzed. Let's explore some of the ways their lives can be changed by research.

Scientists have studied animals for many years in order to increase their knowledge.

Small Size, Big Impact

Some animals' lives can be changed by very tiny pieces of research equipment, such as a radio tracking collar. This is a device that researchers put around an animal's neck so they can monitor the animal's location. Radio tracking collars can do an amazing number of things using a Global Positioning System, or GPS. This system permits the collar to pinpoint an animal's exact longitude and latitude at any time, day or night, for researchers. Other sensors can monitor the temperature and light conditions of the animal's surroundings, and even the direction and speed at which an animal is traveling! Some tracking devices that are now available require only a set of AA batteries, which is no more than a regular flashlight uses.

The use of tracking devices on wild animals has exploded with improvements in technology.

Even with the convenience and capabilities of today's radio tracking collars, there are still problems that researchers need to address. First of all, the collar has to be placed on the animal. Secondly, the animal has to continue wearing the collar for it to work successfully.

This can lead to unintended consequences. What if the animal is accidentally hurt while the collar is being put in place? What if the collar irritates the animal's skin? What if the collar's electrical signals harm the animal? What if other animals are attracted to the collar and then attack the animal that is wearing it? What if the animal chews the collar off, or the collar gets lost in some other way? What if the collar is damaged and harms the animal in some way? How is the collar retrieved without harming the animal? As tiny as a radio tracking collar is, it can still lead to an ordeal for the animal wearing it.

Seeing It Their Way

Some people may already consider GPS-based tracking devices to be primitive when compared to the latest equipment. For instance, researchers are now placing "critter cams" on Alaskan brown bear cubs to visually record their movements. These devices are actually tiny video cameras that contain microphones to record sound and other tools that gather data similar to that gathered by radio tracking collars, data such as temperature and time.

Critter cams allow researchers to have the same view that the cubs themselves have, wherever the cubs may go. The cameras have become so popular that researchers have even placed them on marine animals, data such as marlin, humpback whales, monk seals, and sperm whales.

As advanced as the critter cam is, it still has to be attached to a collar that gets placed around the animal's neck. According to researchers, when the collar containing the critter cam is first placed around a cub's neck, the cub's mother will make a point of inspecting it. After the mother has determined that the collar is harmless, she usually ignores it.

Some researchers are already confident that the collar has no effect on behavior. As with the GPS tracking devices, however, we still do not know how critter cams will ultimately impact animals' lives.

Recording equipment, such as "critter cams," can give researchers a unique perspective on how animals live.

Smile for the Camera

There are less intrusive ways for researchers to study wild animals, as is the case with conducting photo surveys. With photographs, the animals do not need to be given drugs to put them temporarily to sleep, a necessary step for researchers using radio tracking collars or critter cams. By using photography, researchers do not need to worry about equipment that has been placed on animals breaking down or animals being harmed by the equipment in any way.

On the African grasslands, photo surveys have become important for measuring the populations of animals such as the wild African dog. Each wild African dog has a unique color pattern on its fur, which means that individual dogs can be easily tracked using photos.

Photo surveys are conducted from a distance, but they still may affect animal behavior. For instance, what if the flash used for a night photo causes the wild dogs to panic or become confused? On the African grasslands, a camera flash might be the only source of light for miles around. If the wild dogs become overly excited, they might pose a threat to the researcher photographing them. The flash from the camera might frighten the wild dogs so that they run away before the entire group can be photographed. Even researchers conducting simple photo surveys must consider the impact on animals' lives.

Researchers look for less disruptive ways to observe and learn about animals.

Photos of African wild dogs are critical for researchers studying their populations.

Call of the Wild

Researchers have other techniques for counting wild animal populations aside from taking photographs. For example, they can use sounds to conduct population surveys on the African spotted hyena. Spotted hyenas are known to be attracted to certain sounds, and they are especially drawn to the sound of a wounded wildebeest calf, since these are hyenas' favorite prey. Hyenas are also lured by the sounds of other hyenas feeding, or of lions fighting or quarreling over territory. Researchers play recordings of those sounds to attract hyenas for study.

Hyenas can be attracted by sound recordings from as far away as 3.5 kilometers, or two miles. Researchers play the recordings for thirty minutes at a time, from one of ten different stations that have been set up. The stations are spaced ten kilometers, or six miles, apart to avoid overlap that might confuse the hyenas.

Even this simple trick, however, may pose a threat to the animal if it causes a change in the hyenas' behavior. If the sounds are played so much that they become a permanent part of the hyenas' existence, the hyenas may start ignoring them. There is a particular chance of this happening if the hyenas learn that there is no food to be had, despite what the sounds indicate. Such trickery might lead to confusion and frustration for the hyenas.

Scientists sometimes record the sounds of wildebeests to attract hyenas.

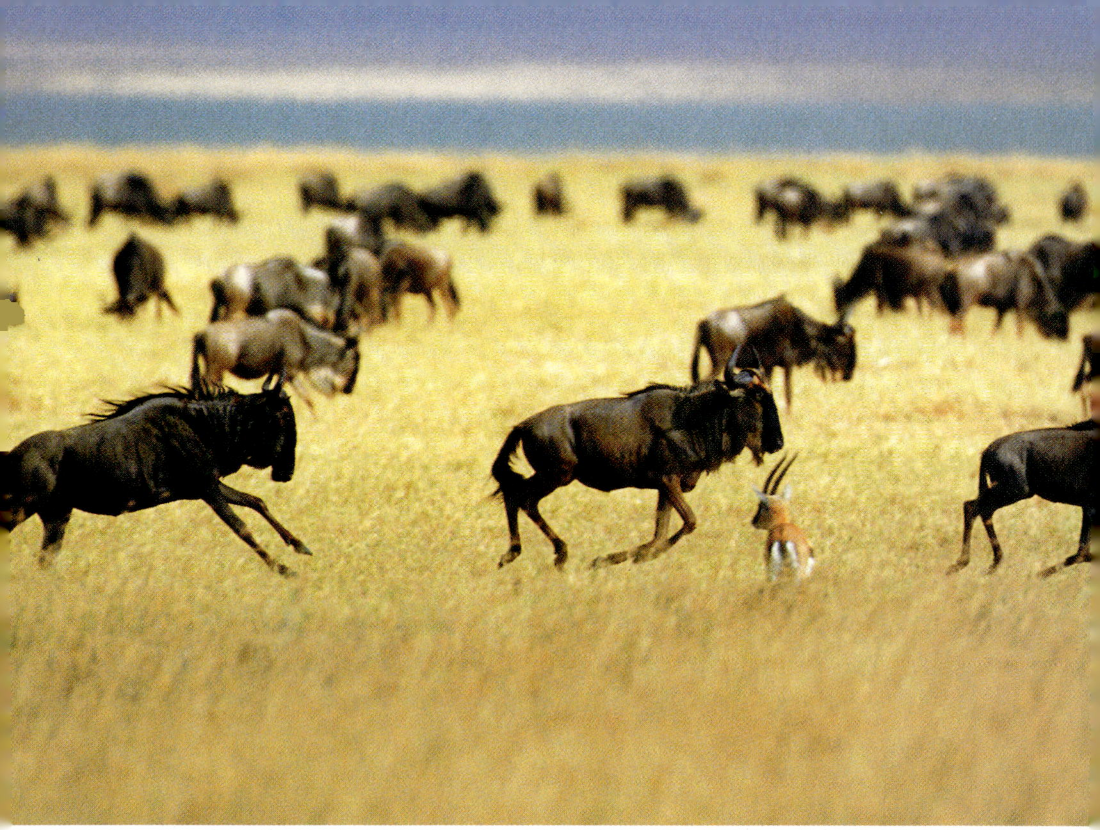

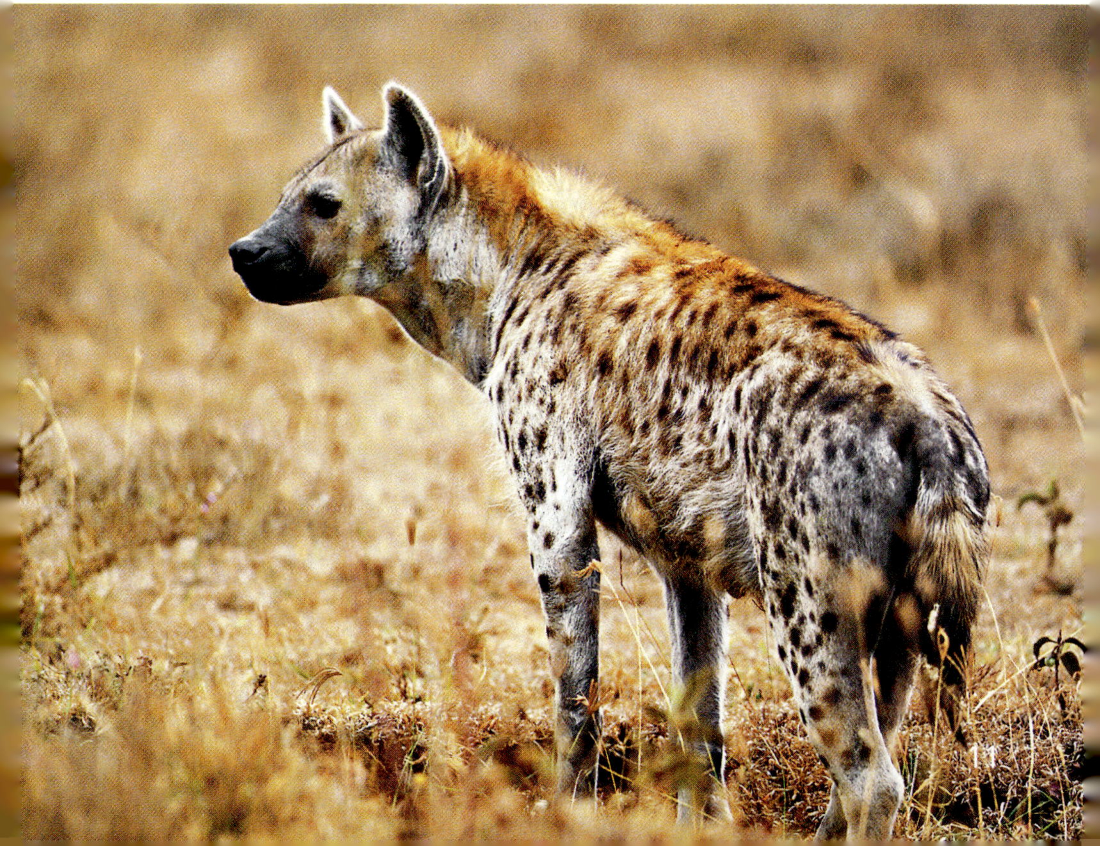

Studying the Nests of Prairie Ducks

Sometimes researchers need to get a little closer to study certain animals, such as nesting prairie ducks. In the case of these animals, researchers conduct something called a "cable-chain drag" to study their populations.

This research method requires two trucks, a "spotter," and a length of chain. The two trucks are spaced well apart, and then are driven parallel to each other at the exact same slow speed across a field, with the chain dragging between them. The spotter is a person who watches for ducks that are forced from their nests by the approaching chain. When a spotter notices a duck fly away, he or she visually marks the spot on the ground, and then goes to that place to find the duck's nest. The goal is to find the nests and take an accurate count of the number of nesting ducks without disturbing them.

Prairie ducks build their nests in fields, as opposed to marshes where many other ducks build nests.

Researchers hope they do not disturb the ducks' nests when they study them.

Destroying the nest is an unfortunate, unintended consequence of this process. Only one person is supposed to visit the nests, so that only one pair of feet tramples the ground. Once researchers are finished, they attempt to return the areas surrounding the nests back to their original state. The reason for this is that predators might be able to spot the ducks' nests more easily if there are signs of disturbance.

Even with all these precautions, some ducks might not return if they see that their nests have been disturbed. More important, the ducks may never return if the dragging operation upsets the nesting process too much. They may start building their nests in fields that humans cannot reach. Worst of all, ducks could get so frightened by the dragging operation that they give up on nesting altogether. Wildlife studies that might seem simple to design can become very complicated when researchers try to anticipate the animals' reactions.

Everyone Loves Pandas — But at What Cost?

American researchers have been studying giant pandas ever since 1972. Currently, there are about 1,600 wild pandas living in the forests of China and 160 captive pandas living in zoos. Because many of the pandas alive today are found in zoos, it is critical that they reproduce successfully. Otherwise, it will be difficult to bring wild panda populations back up to their original levels.

Even though researchers have been studying pandas for more than thirty years, the special problems posed by captivity have still not been totally resolved. For instance, researchers now believe that pandas live best on a bamboo diet. While this isn't a problem for the wild pandas that live in China's bamboo forests, it is for the American pandas that are thousands of miles away from those forests. Their bamboo has to be grown here, or shipped here at great cost. If the bamboo is shipped here, it might lose essential nutrients en route; but if it's grown here, it might not have the same special qualities as Chinese bamboo.

The problems with diets of captive pandas, while significant, still aren't nearly as critical as the problems with panda breeding. Currently, researchers are studying a whole range of factors that might help or hinder the mating and birth of pandas in zoos, including the need for companionship.

Pandas are adored by zoos' visitors, but the lives of wild pandas are at risk.

Researchers are trying to figure out whether pandas prefer to be indoors or outdoors during certain times of the day or year. They are also trying to find out which trees pandas prefer for climbing. In the wild, these problems take care of themselves, but in order to create a successful panda sanctuary, researchers need clues as to what pandas like best. The preferences of pandas are particularly hard to determine, so researchers face a tough task that requires patience and perseverance.

An Unusual Scent

Not all captive animals are as picky as pandas. For instance, researchers seeking an effective way of drawing cheetahs to camera traps in the wild recently stumbled across a strange fact—it turns out that female cheetahs love the smell of a certain kind of men's cologne. When the cologne was sprayed around the habitat of female cheetahs in zoos, they would immediately seek out the source of its smell, and then roll, paw, and rub on the area where the cologne was sprayed. The female cheetahs liked the scent so much that they would even defend the area against approaching males by chasing them off. What could be so attractive about the cologne?

Female cheetahs liked the cologne's smell so much that they defended areas that had been sprayed with it.

Researchers now think that the female cheetahs are attracted to the cologne because it has an odor similar to ones that occur naturally in the wild. In this case, it looks like a win-win situation—the cheetahs like the smell, and it seems to pose no threat to them.

There is still the potential for some problems, though. First of all, what if the cheetahs become unhappy when the cologne's odor disappears? What if the cheetahs are introduced back into the wild, expecting the same cologne smell but unable to locate it? In the end, there will always be some risk involved in using the cologne with the cheetahs because it is an artificial product, so no smell in the wild will ever be able to exactly mimic the smell of the men's cologne.

Pavlov: The First Animal Behaviorist

Ivan Petrovich Pavlov, a Russian physiologist who lived from 1849 to 1936, brought animal research into the modern era with his fascinating studies. During the 1890s, Pavlov was experimenting with dogs' digestive systems, and this pioneering work eventually won him a prestigious award called the Nobel Prize in 1904.

During those experiments, Pavlov noticed that his dogs would start salivating as soon as they saw the person who fed them. In fact, the dogs would begin to drool even if their feeder had no food for them. Pavlov realized that it was enough for the dogs to simply see the person responsible for their feeding in order for them to start salivating. But could this reaction be changed in any way?

Pavlov wanted to know what kinds of stimulating things would cause his dogs to salivate. Knowing that they started salivating because they expected meat, Pavlov began placing meat powder on their tongues. But just before the dogs received the powder, Pavlov rang a bell. Eventually, after the dogs had repeatedly heard the ringing bell, Pavlov stopped giving them any meat powder. Even without the powder, the dogs would still salivate when they heard the bell! Pavlov's discovery of how the dogs' behavior could be altered became known as Pavlovian conditioning.

Pavlov's experiments gave us insight into animal — and human — behavior.

Ivan Pavlov won the Nobel Prize for his groundbreaking studies on animal behavior.

Beyond Pavlov: Dolphins and Operant Conditioning

The implications of Pavlov's studies were enormous because he had proved that if a dog is repeatedly presented with a stimulus (the bell) and its consequence (the meat powder), the dog will begin to link the stimulus with the reward. The dog becomes trained, or conditioned, to expect the reward whenever the stimulus happens, based on its previous experience. What Pavlov demonstrated is that dogs can learn from experience and adapt their behavior based on it.

Of course, dogs are not the only animals that can learn behaviors. One animal that has proved to be an extremely capable learner is the dolphin. Today, scientists expand on Pavlov's principles, using a type of teaching called operant conditioning to train and study dolphins.

The main idea behind operant conditioning is that if an animal performs a behavior, and if the consequences of that behavior are pleasing to the animal, then the animal will probably repeat the behavior. A scientist who wants to train a dolphin to perform a certain behavior will reward the dolphin when it performs that behavior correctly. Over time, the dolphin will learn to expect the reward as a consequence of the behavior. The result is that the dolphin will be more likely to perform the behavior frequently, so that it can receive its reward.

In operant conditioning, the reward that the animal receives is called a positive reinforcer. In this picture, the trainer uses fish as a positive reinforcer to encourage the dolphin to perform the correct behavior.

What kinds of rewards do dolphin trainers use? Like every person, every dolphin has unique tastes. At SeaWorld parks around the country, the most frequent reward for dolphins is food. However, some dolphins also respond well to touching or rubdowns, while others like to be squirted with water, and some even like to play with ice or floating toys. It is important to note that scientists at SeaWorld never punish an animal for incorrect behavior, nor do they force an animal to perform any task. Their teaching is based on only encouragement and rewards.

Dolphins and Humans Learn from Each Other

Both scientists and dolphins benefit from training. For example, a scientist may train a dolphin to move into certain positions during veterinary exams, which makes it easier for the vet to observe the dolphin's health, so both the vet and the dolphin benefit. Also, in the process of training, scientists learn a lot about dolphin intelligence and behavior, and new knowledge about dolphins is a benefit. Finally, trained dolphins present an opportunity for scientists to educate the public. When a dolphin entertains visitors by showing off the tricks it has learned, it is not only fun, but it also raises public awareness about dolphins, their intelligence, and their abilities.

It is possible that training dolphins has some negative effects that scientists have not yet discovered. However, the more scientists learn about dolphins, the more they will be able to help them. Scientists hope that the work of these animals and their trainers will ultimately benefit all dolphins, both captive and wild.

Many people come away from dolphin presentations knowing more about the needs of dolphins and other vulnerable creatures.

The Future

Scientists have studied many animals in many different ways over the years. However, while we have already learned much, we still have a lot more to learn.

Many scientists study animals because they have a great love for the environment, or because they want to help both animals and humans. However, as we have seen, people may also cause changes in animals' lives through their research. Whether through critter cams, colognes, or conditioning, animals are affected by our actions.

For the most part, humans cannot communicate with animals, so we can never know for sure how our behavior affects them. As we move into the future, we must listen to scientists' recommendations about animals and the environment. And we must make sure scientists balance the benefits of their work with its possible consequences.

Glossary

captive *adj.* kept in confinement.

companionship *n.* friendly feeling among companions; fellowship.

existence *n.* condition of being.

ordeal *n.* a severe test or experience.

primitive *adj.* very simple, such as people had in early history.

sanctuary *n.* a place of refuge or protection.

stimulating *adj.* lively; engaging.